# On A Bench of Wood

## Reflections of God's Grace

DARYL MADDEN

Liguori

LIGUORI, MISSOURI

Imprimi Potest
Harry Grile, CSsR, Provincial
Denver Province, The Redemptorists

Published by Liguori Publications
Liguori, Missouri 63057

To order, call 800-325-9521
www.liguori.org

Library of Congress Cataloging-in-Publication Data

Madden, Daryl.
  On a bench of wood : reflections of God's grace / by Daryl
Madden. -- 1st ed.
    p. cm.
  ISBN 978-0-7648-2153-0
  1. Meditations. I. Title.
  BV4832.3.M3155 2012
  242--dc23

                         2012013218

Liguori Publications, a nonprofit corporation, is an apostolate
of the Redemptorists. To learn more about the Redemptorists,
visit Redemptorists.com.

Printed in the United States of America
16 15 14 13 12  /  5 4 3 2 1
First Edition

*To Sister Mary Ellen,*
*who sees with joyful eyes and*
*listens with a compassionate heart,*
*and whose spirit guides with wisdom*
*rooted in an enduring, grateful heart,*
*radiating the love of our Savior.*

# Contents

# Introduction

I am not a religious. I am not a theologian. I am not even a writer.

Several years ago I'd have described myself as a good Christian: I went to church, I prayed most nights, and compared to others I was a good person. But I felt a constant drawing, a need to do more.

I now realize what a shallow spiritual life that was and how much I was missing—how God wants so much more and that, if we take little steps forward in faith, he will lead us into knowing him on a more intimate level.

One Lent I decided that, rather than watching twenty minutes of the *Today* show while eating my morning cereal, I would go for a walk in the woods away from the noise and daily distractions. I would totally give the time to having a conversation with God.

I quickly realized that this time would be useless unless I was completely honest, so I began with thoughts of "I don't think I really love you." And God took me by the hand and showed me his beauty, comfort, and love. I took the time to stop, sit, wonder, open my eyes and ears, and give the thought to God.

Some days I'd get a thought and just have to write it down. This book contains forty-five of those reflections organized by theme: Love, Purpose, Refocus, Grace, Transformation, Surrender, Trust, Brokenness, Hope, and Beauty. My prayer is that you will open your mind and heart, take a step toward Christ, ask him to change you, and have the faith to persevere and trust in him. This is the greatest lesson I've learned: to take time each day, set aside time to be—just *be*—with God.

Take your time with this book. Read it slowly. Use each reflection to begin your time alone with God, either in a pew before Christ or away from the distractions of daily life.

One amazing aspect of God is that he is always available. There are billions of us, and he wants to be with each of us at every moment. He's not only available—he's *fully present*:

*Come to me.*
*I am here.*
*I accept, I forgive, I cherish.*

*In the garden of my safety*
*of holy intimacy,*
*take off your cloak and be.*

*With eternal ears,*
*with endless compassion*
*and infinite love,*

*I am fully present for you.*

God doesn't focus on how you say the words or how you pray; it's the desire or intent of your heart he delights in. So often we think our prayers are meaningless, that God doesn't care, or that we can just pray later. But the creator of the universe is waiting right now, fully present for you.

# Love

Isn't the need to love and to be loved ingrained in the deepest part of our being? Love—isn't that who God is?

And that is where we begin.

Knowing to our core that God loves us is the foundation of our Christian faith. Our world constantly bombards us: *you're not good enough, you're not smart enough, you're not beautiful enough, you're not rich enough, you're not important.*

But, as a wise person once said, "God made you, and God is no dummy."

Our God is love. God loves you, he delights in you, and you are precious to him. Once I saw a newspaper photo of a house covered with thousands of Christmas lights. I thought about all the cost and work someone had put into the house in that photo.

The next morning I went for a walk to spend time with God. The sun was just rising, and each blade of grass in the field was covered in frost. The sun reflected off each blade in an incredible display of sparkling light. As I moved through the field, the bright, pure light reflected in new ways. In just one morning, in just these few moments in just this one little place in all the world, God created this magnificent display.

I've always loved to see the sun shining on water—there's something so special about one light reflecting in so many ways and in so many moments.

*Sunlight dancing on the water*
*playfully brings joy to my soul.*
*Brilliant flashes of pure light*
*sparkle in infinite ways,*
*each one bringing a gift of love to the world.*
*The sun, the water, and the reflection,*
*the Father, the Son, and the Holy Spirit,*
*drawing me into their love.*

I always pause to appreciate moments of sunlight on the water, my thoughts turning to the millennia it took to get to that point: the creation of the sun, the aligning of the solar system, the formation of glaciers, the rain that fell hundreds of miles away that filled the river. And the words came to me: "I would do this all for you."

Physical creation is just a simple action for God. And it's even more amazing that in the ultimate act of humility, grace, and love, God sent his son to us. Even more than that, Jesus lived in perfect obedience to his Father and was crucified for the forgiveness of our sins, all out of love for each of us.

The world bombards us with negative thoughts, but any thought that derails us from the knowledge that God does love us is from the evil one, so it's a constant effort to remind ourselves of the truth.

Just be present for God—be available for him. Just sit in his presence and be with him to develop the practice of letting you be loved. Once we set our foot on that path, everything else can grow out of it.

# And Still…

We tend to think of the people in the Bible as different from us, and in a way they were. But we have the same humanity, the same struggles, and the same God.

Let's bring ourselves into that connection with them. Think of the soldier who nailed Jesus' hands to the cross. Do we think of him as evil? Do we hate him? What brought him to that point? Was he unloved as a child? Was he a faithful soldier just following commands? Was he afraid to say no? Did he not connect with Jesus?

Do I fall into any of those categories?

I can't imagine that in his contact with our Savior he didn't come away changed, the blood of Jesus spilled on his hands.

And still Jesus loved him. Jesus wanted him to spend eternity with him. Even though he performed an act of cruelty, Jesus still loved him.

*I raise the mallet in the air;*
*I strike the nail into your hand;*
*I turn my head;*
*I keep my hands in my pockets—*
*and still you love me.*

*I blend into the crowd, saying,*
*"I do not know him";*
*I disappear inside*
*as I laugh at the joke—*
*and still you forgive me.*

*My stomach yearns*
*with the crowd on the hill;*
*I hold open my hands*
*as I say amen—*
*and still you feed me.*

*I fight through the crowd;*
*I reach out to touch your cloak;*
*I block out the world;*
*I pray with clenched hand—*
*and still you heal me.*

*Our hearts they did burn*
*as he spoke to us on the path;*
*a friend gives advice,*
*a message of peace—*
*and still you walk beside me.*

*I fill another basket*
*with fish bones and scraps of bread;*
*my son hugs his grandma*

*for the freshly baked cookies—*
*and still your grace overflows.*

*I am transfixed by your words*
*as their true meaning sets in;*
*I read the same words*
*and new meanings spring forth—*
*and still you teach me.*

*She smiles as she looks me in the eye*
*and says, "Do whatever he tells you";*
*I roll the bead in my fingers*
*as I ask her to pray for me now—*
*and still she leads me to you.*

*I never look back*
*as I leave my nets and boat behind;*
*I answer the need*
*as I make the time—*
*and still you transform me.*

*You are the same*
*then as now;*
*you are the same*
*forever—*
*and in this stillness, we are one.*

# My Rock

Initially it was easy for me to say I'd go for a walk on a beautiful spring day, and when torrential cold spring rains came, I was tempted to stay inside. But a big part of the Christian life is perseverance, so I bundled up and went out. As I walked in the drenching rain, portions of Matthew 7:24–25 came to me:

*Everyone then who hears these words of mine and acts on them will be like a wise man who built his house on rock. The rain fell, the floods came, and the winds blew and beat on that house, but it did not fall, because it had been founded on rock.*

In so many situations I try to be strong, to handle things on my own and only bother God when I really need him. But God *wants* us to turn to him. Anger, bitterness, joy, stress, loneliness, being scared—these are thoughts God wants us to share with him. He wants to be involved, to be part of our lives, to show his love, to grow our faith in him. We must cling to him as though he were our only hope.

Building on this relationship, we are able to share with others as Jesus calls us to do. Telling stories of how God worked in your life—*that* is sharing your faith.

*In the turmoil of the sea, I find safety on my rock.*
*In the winds of the storm, I find shelter by my rock.*
*In the heat of the fire, I climb upon my rock.*
*In the threat of the enemy, I hide under my rock.*
*In the dark of the night, I find comfort in my rock.*

*I cling to my rock.*
*Letting go, I realize my rock is clinging to me.*
*And having persevered, I am able to share my rock.*

# Old Chapel

I love to go to churches I've never been to, especially when no one else is around and I have the empty, silent church to myself.

After a few minutes of silence, I begin thinking of the parents, grandparents, and teenagers who have come here in desperation. They needed help for the laid-off spouse, for the grandchild turning to drugs. They needed consolation for a lost loved one. Their lives were forever altered by this simple act of faith.

God's compassion for them overwhelms me. But most of all it affects me, how little faith I had (have). When I pray, I hope God answers my prayers on a chance.

But then, in the words of Matthew 17:20, it is that "little faith" that matters. He said,

*For truly I tell you, if you have faith the size of a mustard seed, you will say to this mountain, "Move from here to there," and it will move; and nothing will be impossible for you.*

The people who were here before had that faith when they approached God. I felt just how grateful they were and how grateful I am that our loving God shares in our troubles and humanity.

*In this old, dark, musty chapel,*
*a warm light glows.*

*How many worries have sat in this seat?*
*Were they greater than yours?*
*How many prayers were placed at your feet?*
*Were they not answered by you?*
*How many hearts have entered in fear?*
*Were they not consoled by you?*
*How many minds have been opened here?*
*Were they not guided by you?*

*How many souls have been touched in this place?*
*Are they not in glory with you?*
*How silly we are, how eternal are you.*
*How little I am, how great are you.*
*I place my soul in your care.*

*I rejoice with those souls in offering my praise:*
*How truly merciful and loving are you.*

# Living Now

It was a beautiful warm Saturday, the sun was shining, the stream was flowing, flowers were blooming. I realized just how wonderful this moment was and how much of our lives are consumed by worries, obligations, and perceptions.

Jesus is a God of the moment. He saw who we could become. He knew our purpose was in building the kingdom of God. He didn't hold the shame of the past over our heads.

He is present for us now. How much better my life would be if I let go of my baggage and lived in the *present* of Jesus.

*Oh to live in the spiritual moment of now,*
*where memory bears no grudges,*
*wants bear no need,*
*time knows no rush,*
*acceptance is given,*
*joy is spread,*
*love is now.*

# Walls

We live through trial, pain, rejection, failure, and being unloved. These experiences build a protection of walls, like calluses.

Christian life is unity, inclusion, connecting, and love. The walls we build keep us from those connections. Until we realize that to fully experience the Christian life, the walls must be torn down, we're held prisoners by our own fault. These walls don't come down easily; only by God and the nudging of the Holy Spirit can these be eroded.

This is a prayer for that help. God will be with us on this journey. He will encourage us, and we will see the light of the fruits of this effort.

*In the house that is my soul,*
*many walls have I constructed*
*through fear, through hurt, with bias—*
*some unknowingly—*
*all without the hand of God.*

*They offer no protection,*
*only barriers that keep me in and*
*screens that distort the perspective,*
*blocking the view.*

*Through the love of the Savior*
*in the silence of the unknown,*
*mortar crumbles, walls dismantle,*
*windows are wiped clean.*

*Light brightens darkened corners.*
*Blocked opportunities now are seen.*
*Fullness is glimpsed as vision is restored*
*only through the love of the Creator.*

# Purpose

If I met Jesus in person, what would I ask him? "Are you real?" "Do you really love me?" If those questions were answered, would my next question be, "What is my purpose?"

The textbook answer is to know, to love, and to serve God. But what would that look like on a day-to-day basis? What great things would you want me to do?

Each day God gives us what we need. God prepares our day with physical, material, and spiritual blessings. He surrounds us with beauty. He places people in our path. He presents challenges that allow us to grow.

Are we aware of God's presence in those things? Each day God gives us opportunities to grow in faith, trust, and love in him. Each day we mess up, and the next day he changes everything and constructs new opportunities for us.

# Who Is God Sending to Me?

God allows us to grow in infinite ways through the people we encounter. We tend to view those encounters through our eyes only. What can *I* get out of the relationship, how can they serve *me*, how did they offend *me*, how can *I* feel better about *myself* because they are less than *I*?

Each encounter is an opportunity. God places these people in my path for a reason. I pray that I'm not too busy, too selfish, or too afraid to embrace the encounter. Let me be fully present for them.

*Who is God sending to me?*
*How can I help—*
*help build the kingdom, help strengthen his love?*
*Lord, grant me wisdom.*

*Where is the question?*
*How can I listen—*
*listen for the need, listen for the reason?*
*Help me ask the right questions.*
*Lord, grant me peace.*

*How can I receive—*
*receive your lesson, receive their love?*
*Help me see you in them.*

*Help me see beyond the mask.*
*Lord, grant me humility.*

*What does God want me to do?*
*How can I bring peace—*
*peace of Christ, peace of love?*
*How can I keep myself out of the way?*
*Help me see clearly not what I want,*
*but what you want.*
*Lord, grant me love.*

*How can I share—*
*share his joy, share his gifts?*
*Help me be your true servant.*
*Help me bring Christ to others.*
*Lord, grant me joy.*

*You have entrusted me with this opportunity.*
*You have empowered me,*
*for you have filled me—*
*you are in me, and I am in you.*
*You have blessed me with your grace and love.*
*This is not about me.*
*It's about a servant*
*going about his Master's business.*
*Help me go in peace to love and serve the Lord.*

# Help Me

Too often we think we *should* do this or *should* do that or *should* pray more or *should* volunteer more.

As my friend Sister Mary Ellen advises, "We shouldn't *should* all over ourselves." When we have the *should* attitude, we place the center of our purpose on ourselves.

In reality, we can't do anything by ourselves. If we shift that attitude toward God, we will be successful.

*O, my Jesus, help me.*

*Thank you for your humbleness;*
*help me be humble.*
*Thank you for your forgiveness;*
*help me forgive.*
*Thank you for your mercy;*
*help me be merciful.*
*Thank you for your compassion;*
*help me be compassionate.*
*Thank you for your kindness;*
*help me be kind.*
*Thank you for your joy;*
*help me be joyful.*
*Thank you for your love;*
*help me love.*

# Transfer of Hope

I realized one day that I wasn't joyful.

But isn't being joy-filled one of the characteristics of a Christian? Then why wasn't I? Couldn't I will myself to be filled with joy?

And that was the issue: the *I* in that statement. *God* is the source of love and joy. I was making myself the center. How much time do I reflect on what *I* am doing? How much time do I reflect on what *God* is doing? How much time do I take to actually "sit" in the Scriptures?

Going back to joy, could I reflect upon the birth of our Savior?

> *The angel said to them, "Do not be afraid;*
> *for see—I am bringing you good news of great*
> *joy for all the people." Luke 2:10*

*Good news of great joy.* God sent his son to be one of us. Jesus didn't just learn *about* how we live, he *lived* it. He knows our challenges; he knows our pain. Will we take the opportunity to know Jesus?

This is our source of joy. It leads us to proclaim, "Glory to God in the highest!" And we receive peace. Isn't it wonderful to know that upon us God's favor rests?

This is a reflection of surrender, of placing God back in the center. From that center, all things flow.

*I cannot produce joy.*
*I cannot produce peace.*
*I cannot produce love.*

*This doesn't mean I have no hope—*
*just no hope in myself.*
*Transferring the hope to our Lord—*
*these are gifts from our Father.*

*I can turn to God.*
*I can place my requests at Jesus' feet.*
*I can submit my will.*
*I can acknowledge and be grateful for these gifts.*

*And I can share*
*his joy,*
*his peace,*
*his love,*
*and his hope.*

# Grant Me

The key to the spiritual path is God's love—to become aware of it, to acknowledge it, and to accept it. But there are stumbling blocks. First, the insecurities: *What will they think of me? What good can I do? Let someone else do it.* Second, the dangers of that service are the building up of *me.* *I'm* a good person, aren't *I* wonderful, look what people say about *me.*

Allow me to let go. Let the focus be God.

I attended a Christian camp where, despite the hard work and uncomfortable accommodations, everyone was joyful and fulfilled: "Everyone is joyful here because we're doing what God intended."

We think we're doing something for God when we serve others. But in reality, God is giving us an opportunity for the joy found only in him.

*Lord, let me know your love.*
*Help me love you more.*
*Grant me the wisdom to let go*
*so your love may shine through me.*

# May You Find

Every day we have numerous opportunities, decisions, and actions. We're trapped in busy-ness and seem to rush through the day.

Here is a reflection on trying to slow each decision of the day. God calls us to action. He blesses us with being his servant. We're honored to be part of the building of his kingdom.

This is a call to turn to God in all aspects of your day. Too often our hearts become hard, so ask God to help keep your heart and your purpose focused on him.

*When the opportunity arises*
*in the struggles of my loved ones,*
*may you find a generous heart.*

*When my righteousness rises*
*in the face of hurt,*
*may you find a forgiving heart.*

*When I go about my day*
*with the blessings you've bestowed on me,*
*may you find a grateful heart.*

*When I hear your whisper*
*in the noise of the world,*
*may you find a willing heart.*

*When the voice of silence resounds*
*in the teaching of my soul,*
*may you find a pliable heart.*

*When I hold your son*
*in the palm of my hand,*
*may you find an open heart.*

*When I don't know what to do—*
*and even when I do—*
*may I find you.*

# Refocus

When we get caught up in the grind and the momentum of the day overwhelms us, shift the focus from yourself to your relationship with the Father who cherishes us.

When we get caught up in busy-ness, the first thing we tend to do is ask God to solve our problems, to take care of what is needed. We anxiously await a response from God, not remembering he is already there.

We seek, we want, we do. We're driven to fill our needs. When we watch TV, read a paper, go online, or even drive down the road, advertisements place a desire in our mind. But these things never fill or satisfy.

We think our parents, friends, or spouse will fill our needs. And, as they let the Holy Spirit flow through them, God does.

Our thoughts and emotions are gifts from God. God also gave us the gift of free will, so what we do with our emotions is under our control. If someone says something to anger us, we can respond with hate, sink into bitterness, or turn it over to God and respond with love and compassion.

Wanting to respond that way is one thing, doing it is another. No wonder God gives us so much practice with those situations.

We need to start with God. We need to know God can meet our needs. We need to spend time with God, pouring out our needs and problems. We need to spend time alone with God to let him console, heal, and love us.

# My Own Little Swamp

Time and again, I find myself worn down, feeling wronged, edging into bitterness, and feeling stressed.

One morning while sitting by a creek, trying to spend time with God but unable to let go of my daily troubles, I saw animal tracks in the mud. That was how I felt—stepped on and stuck in the mud.

But right next to the mud was a sparkling stream. The water was flowing over rocks and stones and making a beautiful splashing noise. I saw the sun shining through the tall trees. I realized how little I was. I realized God was there just waiting, not telling me how selfish I was or how blessed I was in so many ways. He was just there, smiling and full of compassion. I wanted to jump into his arms—Jesus, the river of grace.

*Here I sit in my own little swamp,*
*festering in my needs and wants,*
*stuck in my self-pity and worries,*
*suffocating in my humanity.*

*Help me raise my eyes to you.*
*Pull me from the mud and lift me up.*
*Bring me to the shore*
*and let me dive into you.*

*Allow me to float in your river of grace,*
*bobbing and drifting in your warm embrace,*
*feeling the light of your love shining on me,*
*drawing me ever closer.*

*I don't ask to be freed from trials and challenges—*
*only to place them in your control,*
*always from your perspective,*
*seeing everything through you.*

*O Father, you are the way.*
*Help me focus on you.*
*Help me just let go*
*and trust and rejoice in you.*

# Prayer for the
# Life in the Spirit Group

God presents us with opportunities to grow in holiness, to grow in our faith, and to grow closer to him. As Matthew 7:7–8 says,

*Ask, and it will be given to you; search, and you will find; knock, and the door will be opened for you.*
*For everyone who asks receives, and everyone who searches finds, and for everyone who knocks, the door will be opened.*

Most of the time I know when I'm seeking, but when should I knock? How many times are we confronted with a choice? How many excuses do we have for not taking the brave step? How many times do we say we don't have time?

God rewards little steps forward. They allow God to open doors for us. Think about the people stepping forward. Think about the blessed, faithful, holy people who host seminars so we might learn. Think about what you get for attending.

*Holy Spirit, enjoy the willingness of these souls*
*who are precious to you.*
*Through Jesus Christ I ask you to…*

*enlighten their spirit,*
*enhance their vision,*
*enrich their hearing,*
*encourage their heart,*
*impassion their souls,*
*empower their being;*

*breathe on them,*
*bathe them in your light,*
*burn in their hearts,*
*flood them with your gifts;*

*spring forth a new being who*
*is aware of God's presence,*
*thirsts for his Word,*
*seeks his guidance,*
*serves his purpose,*
*spreads his love.*

# Senses of the Soul

In sitting and being with God, I've come to know that words can't always capture true thoughts and feelings. How limited is my vision if I believe the only senses are the five human ones?

Initially I felt *I* had to fill the void of silence in my conversation with God. When people said they heard from God, I wondered, did they actually hear God speak, did they *feel* God speak? What did that actually mean?

I realized that conversation with God is communication that can't be defined by the senses that have been defined by science. The spiritual senses are much more important and harder to refine.

This communication isn't something I do. All I do is let go and let God do.

I love the idea of that pure point of light deep within us. That's how I felt about the senses of the soul.

*Close your eyes and see,*
*quiet your ears and hear,*
*silence your mouth and speak—*
*cultivating the senses of the soul.*

*Open your heart,*
*free your mind,*
*release your being—*
*letting prayer happen.*

*Focus on the pure light of the soul,*
*let it consume and grow,*
*let it spread—*
*connecting with the Supreme Presence of love.*

# Refocusing

We live in a stressful world. Jesus urged us time and again not to worry. We try, but it always seems to creep back in. Our prayer time with God is a wonderful time to combat stress.

This is a reflection of recommitment, of saying that I am not God. This is a prayer of letting go and sitting in the light of God.

*The poison of stress and worry*
*drip off my shoulders,*
*falling into you,*
*glimpsing the vision,*
*gaining the perspective of truth,*
*turning over the reins,*
*refocusing on love,*
*basking in light.*

# Which

Sitting by a peaceful stream, I was distracted by the loud rush of traffic. I was irritated until I realized the traffic didn't control me.

*I* let myself be irritated. We go through our day thinking about what the *world* does to us, when it's *us* doing it to us.

I have a choice. I decide how I interpret words and sights and feelings. Will I take the easy route and follow the crowd? Will I always do something simply because it's the way it's always been done? Will I always respond in the way I've been programmed? Will I focus on being more aware?

I love this story of Mother Teresa. A writer was following her through the streets of Calcutta when she seemingly disappeared. Then she reappeared holding a sick, starving person. No one else had noticed this person. She was aware, she had a purpose, she paid attention. Will I follow the crowd or follow God's path for me?

*Which will I hear?*
*The harsh drone of the traffic*
*or the soft gentle sound of the stream?*

*Which shall I walk?*
*The monotonous shuffle of the crowd*
*or the stroll of the gift-bearer?*

*Which shall I cheer?*
*The flash of the famous*
*or the smile of a child?*

*Which will I follow?*
*The arrogance of self*
*or the humbleness of a beggar?*

# Grace

*We tend to expect everything to be perfect,
to go through life without challenges
or difficulties. It is precisely in those
challenges that we encounter God.*

S aint Thérèse of Lisieux said, "Everything is grace." What a wonderful (and humbling) thought. Everything we see, eat, feel, and experience is a gift from God.

Joyful people cultivate a spirit of gratitude. The world tells us we're to be respected and that we're deserving, but we deserve nothing. Let us celebrate the goodness of our loving God by cultivating a grateful heart.

God calls us to be part of his kingdom. How often do we try to build *our* kingdom instead? I can give God nothing except my time, my intent to be with him, and my will at that moment. I realize my nothingness. But in that nothingness I'm connected to God, who is all love, all beauty, all wisdom, owner of eternity.

# And I Fall…

We're so conditioned by our world that we must be perfect, we must be successful, and we must not fail. Our self-worth is determined by our "successes."

But we're *not* perfect, and we *will* fail. Where does that leave us? Fortunately, God doesn't think that way. He wants us to grow into holiness. In our failings and successes, we turn to God.

Often we ask *why*. It's good to question and to ponder. In our earthly lives, sometimes we find out why and sometimes we don't. The key is to trust and to know that God is in control and that God is good. Aren't we blessed that when we fall, God is always there, always compassionate, always loving?

Let God reign in the center of our being by turning to him in all aspects of our day.

*I try and I try.*
*But I slip back into the same sin.*
*And I fall…*
*into your arms, and I learn of your mercy.*

*She is very sick.*
*The doctors don't know what to do.*
*And I fall…*
*into your arms, and I learn of your comfort.*

*I am so busy.*
*There is no time to pray.*
*And I fall…*
*into your arms, and I learn of your peace.*

*It cannot be done.*
*I just don't know what to do.*
*And I fall…*
*into your arms, and I learn of your grace.*

*I see all the suffering.*
*What can I do?*
*And I fall…*
*into your arms, and I learn of your compassion.*

*I am afraid.*
*I do not know the next step.*
*And I fall…*
*into your arms, and I learn of your gentleness.*

*It makes no sense.*
*Why should this happen?*
*And I fall…*
*into your arms , and I learn of your plan.*

*My prayers are so dry.*
*It feels as if you're not there.*
*And I fall…*
*into your arms, and I learn of your faithfulness.*

*I have been hurt.*
*I am so bitter.*
*And I fall…*
*into your arms, and I learn of your humility.*

*I make the donation.*
*I cannot afford it.*
*And I fall…*
*into your arms, and I learn of your generosity.*

*It is so beautiful.*
*I am filled with awe.*
*And I fall…*
*into your arms, and I learn of your beauty.*

*I read of your Word.*
*I sit in your silence.*
*And I fall...*
*into your arms, and I learn of your love.*

*I lend a hand to my brother.*
*I see the smile on his face.*
*And I fall...*
*into your arms, and I learn of your joy.*

*Your body is lifted up before my eyes.*
*I say amen.*
*And I fall...*
*into your arms, and I learn of your passion.*

*I cherish my memories and regret my mistakes.*
*I close my eyes at last.*
*And I fall...*
*into your arms, and I learn of your glory.*

# A Connection of Grace

We sometimes feel we have to do it all and sometimes feel we *can* do it all. How quickly we learn we can't—like when someone asks me to show him the color blue. I dig around in a junk drawer, pull out an old ragged crayon and paper, and scribble. We ask God to show us the color blue, and he gives us the sky.

We don't want to cultivate the spirit that we are no good or worthless. We need to be reminded that all God has to offer is available to us—we just need to ask.

The next time someone asks me to show him the color blue, what if instead of coloring, I bring my friend outside and show him the sky and what God gives us.

We have the opportunity to be part of God's ocean of love. What an incredible gift to be connected to God's grace.

*A connection of being—*
*of nothingness with all*

*A connection of love—*
*of a drop into the ocean*

*A connection of openness—*
*of a window to the sky*

*A connection of spirit—*
*of a breath to the wind*

*A connection of grace—*
*of an ember to a blaze*

*A connection of time—*
*of a moment into eternity*

# A Moment of Light

I was praying on an incredibly beautiful summer morning. It was like falling into beauty. It was a glimpse of heaven. God's love is too powerful for us to handle—it has to be given to us in little drops.

I saw how trite earthly issues are. Reason screamed, "You're crazy! You're imagining this!" But my heart told me differently.

When you experience gifts from God that reason says are crazy or made up, hold them. Cherish them.

*The intense blinding of pure grace*
*drops me to my knees, filling me with humility.*
*Grasping at the moment, trying to hold on*
*as it slips through my fingers,*
*left empty as it fades,*
*leaving a soul less jagged,*
*a bond made stronger,*
*and a grateful heart.*

# Stop

I'm too busy. I'm running late. I have to take care of the kids. I'm too tired. We brag that we're too busy as though our value is based on how busy we are.

Sometimes a prayer of fifteen seconds can be more powerful than a prayer of an hour. If you're too busy, just stop. Pray, "God, I want to be with you, please turn these ten seconds into much more." God doesn't call us to do a lot; he calls us to be who he made us to be. He wants us to be fully alive.

Say this short prayer throughout the day as a reminder to connect with God, to let him love us in this moment, and to rise into our godly calling.

*Let me be alive in this moment,*
*aware of your presence.*
*Let me be fully present for you,*
*enveloped by your grace,*
*enriched by your love,*
*rising above and into the letting go.*

# Blessed Wisdom

In moments of contemplation of Scripture, thoughts from a friend, or words from a sermon, a message rings true and we realize we need to grow in a certain area. We think about it, it makes sense, and we plan to make the change.

But then we have to put it into practice. Our old self screams in protest. Will we make the change? Sometimes yes, sometimes no. If no, God will continue to give us the opportunity to practice the blessed wisdom he granted us. If yes, we've won a battle against evil and received the gift of joy in the building of God's kingdom.

*And it hangs like a thread*
*waiting to be pulled—*
*the thought that becomes blessed wisdom.*

*And the hurt painfully stings,*
*pride roaring like a lion—*
*exercise waiting to be practiced.*

*And the gift of joy received,*
*acknowledging the light—*
*rejoicing in blessings.*

# Transformation

Time and again we read in Scripture that people are changed after encountering Jesus. How would we become more holy if we spent just a few minutes each day encountering him?

It's hard to read Scripture without thinking about transformation. Christian life *is* transformation. And it's hard (if not impossible) to look around and not see change. Each day the weather changes, the trees change, we physically change. But do we change spiritually? Do we grow? Do we pray *God, please change me?*

Why are we so afraid of change? Look back on some of your most difficult times and challenges. Did you grow from those experiences? Have you used those experiences to help others?

# Good Morning Again

I was sitting, just taking time to see what was in front of me. I thought about what those things brought to me. I thought about how beautiful those gifts were.

I thought about what was on my mind. I thought about what junk it was. What was that worth to God?

God wants to be my best friend. He wants to take away my junk. He wants me to be free. When I empty myself of burdens, sins, and distractions, I see clearly—and what I see is God.

How grateful I am! He replaces my burdens, sins, and distractions with peace, comfort, love, and wisdom. These are the gifts he calls me to share. I leave transformed.

*Good morning again, my child,*
*I greet you with the light of my love.*
*Enjoy the singing praises of the birds as I give you*
*the peace of the stream,*
*the purity of the snow,*
*the faithfulness of the oak,*
*the challenges of the day.*

*Good morning again, my Lord,*
*I feel the warmth of your embrace.*
*Enjoy the willingness of my heart as I give you*
*the distractions of my mind,*
*the failures of my sin,*
*the brashness of my pride,*
*the selfishness of my wants.*

*And we come together in*
*the stillness of my heart,*
*the silence of your wisdom,*
*the peace in my soul,*
*the direction of your purpose,*
*the joy of our friendship.*

*And I leave with*
*your peace,*
*your comfort,*
*your strength,*
*your humility,*
*your grace.*

# Turn to God

God loves us so much that he lets us decide whether to turn to him. He doesn't force us.

The path of transformation turns away from the things of the world. We're to be *in* the world—not *of* it.

Our transformation is a series of little steps. God places opportunities in front of us each day. Will we be aware of them? Will we act on them? Will we move closer to God?

Deciding to answer God's call through the Holy Spirit is a conscious turning toward God—a transformation to holiness.

*Follow the light—*
*and turn your life around.*

*Read the page in Scripture—*
*and turn the words over in your mind.*

*Acknowledge the grace of God—*
*and turn it into faith.*

*See the love around us—*
*and turn it into praise.*

*Stand firm in your faith—*
*and turn the other cheek.*

*Grow closer to our Lord—*
*and turn away from sin.*

*Thwart the spread of bitterness—*
*and turn to forgiveness.*

*Know of his resurrection—*
*and turn to joy.*

*Turn away from darkness—*
*and turn to the light.*

# The Crossing

A work colleague died in a freak accident. On Friday he was at work, and by Sunday he was gone. He loved life—he loved to cook, he loved the outdoors, he loved to build. He connected with everyone from executives to manual laborers.

I never shared my faith with him. Our time on Earth is a blip on the line of eternity. As Christians, our message is to share not the fear of hell, but the joy of heaven.

Fortunately, God is beyond time, and we can always turn to him.

*He was just here, just yesterday.*
*Now he's gone.*
*His faithful mom and his beloved*
*wake in the rising dawn.*

*His good nature left behind,*
*his friends are left to cry,*
*to grieve in sorrow, carry on,*
*and sit and wonder why.*

*His cabin sits in silence.*
*His toys are just a waste.*
*His laughter echoes in the woods.*
*His meals have lost their taste.*

*The passion with which he lived his life,*
*he shares with us this day.*
*We carry him in our hearts,*
*each in our own way.*

*Our prayers eternally pass through time.*
*They're caught with merciful hands*
*by the Father of compassion—*
*we know he understands.*

*As I sat by the stream this morn,*
*in silence I did pray.*
*I raised my head and understood.*
*I knew what God would say:*

*A strong, stout deer gazed at me*
*until he caught my eye.*
*He raised his head in confidence*
*And crossed to the other side.*

# Surrender

Think about receiving Communion. Is your heart open? Do you look forward to receiving him? What if you opened every cell of your being and allowed the miracle of him to transform you?

When I'm feeling stressed, do I surrender to God? When I'm frustrated, do I surrender to God? When I feel guilty, do I surrender to God? When I pray, do I surrender to God? When I'm hurt, do I surrender to God?

We have a blessed opportunity each week at church to prepare for this great celebration. As we go into church, we've had our breakfast, prepared our clothes, and mapped out our schedule. As we enter the church, we see preparation all around us: the choir has practiced, the bulletin is ready, and the lector reads.

But is our soul prepared? Do we enter church with eager anticipation? The more you put into the your worship, the more you get.

# Every Cell

Words can't begin to describe the beauty and privilege of the opportunity to give God all of yourself. We're touched in so many beautiful ways.

As I share in Communion, a line forms. As people approach, they hold out two open hands. Some hands are old and wrinkled, some young and soft, and some hard and callused. Some hands are offered in reverence, some offered in nervousness, and some offered in indifference.

God isn't angry at the indifferent. God encounters us with love, compassion, and hope. God meets us exactly where we are. He gave us his precious son. Jesus blessed us with a customized plan of exactly what we need to grow in holiness.

Everyone approaches Jesus in a different way. Let us approach him with surrender in our hearts.

*O Lord,*
*we remember your perfection at Communion.*
*You are presented before us,*
*and with a simple amen*
*we state our belief*
*that you died for us,*
*all out of love.*

*So fill me, Lord.*
*I open every cell of my body*
*to be permeated by you—*
*to be transformed by you.*

*I hold nothing back.*
*I submit, I surrender, I relent.*
*Be all of me.*

*Be the direction in my feet that guides.*
*Be the warmth in my hands that acts.*
*Be the kindness in my mouth that consoles.*
*Be the patience in my ears that listens.*
*Be the compassion in my eyes that expresses.*
*Be the wisdom in my mind that decides.*
*Be the love in my heart that cares.*

# Decision

........................................................................................................

One day I had to make an important briefing for a customer and his advisors. Our company expert had just left the company, and I had to fill in. I did what I could to prepare, but there was no way to understand everything in a short amount of time.

I was afraid they would ask detailed questions I couldn't answer, so I sat and prayed. The words came: *Do you trust me?*

In the scheme of things, this was small. But if I say I'm Christian and can't trust in Jesus' help with this meeting, when *can* I trust him? What was I afraid of?

*Sitting on the precipice of decision*
*between trusting in self and trusting in God,*
*between pride and surrender,*
*between arrogance and obedience—*
*letting go and falling into his arms,*
*bringing the decision of eternity.*

# Rescue Me

I sat down to pray, but I couldn't concentrate. Thoughts of stress at work, of stress at home, of incompetence, and of what people had done to me as well as bitterness, entitlement, and self-righteousness were raging though my mind.

How could I sit in silence and peace with all my troubles? Was I willing to surrender all of this to God? Do I have a Savior?

*God of light, shine on me*
*and purge this bitter soul*
*of selfishness.*
*Sitting, sulking, searching,*
*mouth yapping, arms flailing—*
*Let me find your hand*
*to pull me out of the muck and*
*rinse me clean from the inside out.*
*Jesus my light,*
*Jesus my God,*
*Jesus my Savior,*
*rescue me.*

# Twilight

The time just after the sun sets is a beautiful closing to the day. It's a time of surrender, a time to reflect on the things I did in service to God and the things I could have done better. It's a time to let all that go and be comforted by the knowledge that God still loves us no matter what we did. It's a time to experience the peace of that love.

*Twilight rests on the horizon,*
*whispering thoughts of letting go,*
*casting away the cares of the day*
*with the setting sun.*
*Emptiness consumes the evening sky.*
*Sparkling points of light and*
*thoughts of insignificance*
*lead to the comforting infinity that surrounds,*
*blanketing our souls.*

# Trust

So often we focus on the problem sitting in front of us at this moment. We think the issue is insurmountable. Is there a problem too big for God?

Trust is one of my biggest challenges. Over and over I've faced problems and worried about them. And over and over, God has resolved them. At the end of a trial, I'm amazed and grateful to God, and I vow that next time I'll trust. I feel God smiling, because he knows it's a process for me.

My good friend Michael says it all comes down to one thing: *Do we really believe?* During an Advent sermon, a pastor discussed Luke 1:37, when the angel came to Mary. He talked about the statement "For nothing will be impossible with God."

Have you ever seen the hand of God? A sick friend is cured. A friend who has lived without faith develops a new relationship with God. A friend with financial troubles loses her job, receives a good severance package, and finds a better job a week later. Is my faith strong enough to trust God through circumstances like these?

Reflection on how God has touched our lives

is wonderful but so small compared to a God who would send his son as a child. *For nothing will be impossible with God.*

I like to reflect on the passage in Matthew 9:27 about the two blind men sitting by the road. They had heard about Jesus. They were hopeful. But Jesus passed them by.

Were they thinking *poor me, Jesus ignored me, I can't even see enough to follow him.* But the blind men followed. They ventured into the unfamiliar house, feeling their way around, probably bumping into things. But they continued.

When they found Jesus, were they afraid to approach him? Because of their trust, perseverance, faith, and hope, Jesus touched them and their eyes were opened.

Would we have had the same trust?

# Deep Silence

I was sitting in an empty church on a workday afternoon. The sun was streaming through the stained-glass windows. I tried to just let go and be enveloped in God's presence and silence. This was a prayer without words—just trying to let go of everything and trust God. So often I pray for people, things I want, and issues to be resolved, but for once I wanted to just give myself to the Lord.

I sometimes feel that in this deep silence, in his presence, my soul is somehow loved and molded outside my knowing. I just put my soul into his hands completely—and trust him.

*Strolling slowly into deep silence,*
*guided by the spirit,*
*falling, slipping,*
*drifting with the Lord in step,*
*drawing deeper,*
*deeper into the unawareness of teaching,*
*floating in peace,*
*soothing the restless heart.*

# Building Trust

Trust cannot be built by just hearing about it or accepting it. Like so many things in the Christian life, it has to be experienced, so we must face trials.

If we continue to turn to the Lord, we will learn to trust. In our storms of trials, hurts, and problems, let our first thoughts be of God.

*The rain pelts,*
*the wind howls,*
*the waves crash.*
*Finding strength in the storm,*
*turning inward toward*
*the one true light,*
*building the core from life's trials*
*brings the external treasure of trust.*

# Ship at Night

I was on a cruise ship with my family. One very black night I went out to the bow of the ship. The wind was whipping in all directions, and I almost went in, but something encouraged me to stay.

The ship seemed to symbolize life. We tend to gravitate toward satisfying our needs and wants, tending to concentrate on our daily needs. But we are part of something much greater than ourselves. God invites us to be part of the building of his kingdom.

Perhaps we should start each day thinking of the greater battle between good and evil and being aware of the part we play in that battle. Are we too comfortable? Do we just follow the routine?

*Ship cruising into the black night,*
*where the ocean of the now*
*disappears into the horizon of what is to be,*
*forging ever onward,*
*the fierce battle is fought in the whipping wind.*
*In the comfort of the hull,*
*passengers concern themselves with the trite,*
*unaware of the true battle that rages in the night.*
*The ship is steady, set upon its course.*
*One must venture into the elements*
*to realize the true greatness of the ship,*
*to join the crew in awareness*
*of the sacrifice and purpose of the way.*

# Comfort Me in Trust

When we pray the Lord's Prayer, how often do we pass over the words "thy will be done on earth as it is in heaven"? How much less worry and stress would we have if we viewed our lives from God's perspective?

Jesus is always by our side, just waiting for us to give our burdens to him. He wants us to share our troubles with him. He wants to be part of our lives.

Will we let him?

*In the midst of my troubles and stress,*
*my Lord,*
*my wishes, hopes, and desires*
*rest in your gracious hands.*
*Help me accept your will and direction.*
*Please come alongside me,*
*my advisor and confidant,*
*my savior and friend,*
*my Lord and my God.*
*Let your will be done.*

# Battle of Will

How often do we pray *Lord, help me more patient; Lord, help me be more kind.* But when we get the opportunity to practice these things, how quickly old patterns and emotions flare.

I pray to be more patient, but there's a new clerk in the grocery checkout line, and I'm in a hurry.

I pray to be more kind, but my spouse snaps at me, and I snap back.

We need to remind ourselves that we're part of a bigger picture: the building of the kingdom of God.

*Within the battle of my will,*
*the loud and boisterous voice of pride*
*fills the decision.*
*In the corner of silence*
*whispers the guidance of the Spirit.*
*On the wind of trust,*
*the whisper floats above.*
*The courageous choice is*
*the foundation of victory.*

# Brokenness

How many of us are spiritually stuck? How often do we feel broken and lost? Where do we go?

The answer is Jesus, and the first step is trust.

David was living in a small assisted-living apartment when I met him. He used a wheelchair because he was partially paralyzed. I was there to teach him to use a computer, but God had other plans for our friendship.

David had been a millionaire with a yacht, a fancy car, a few houses, a wife, and children. He had everything but his faith. He didn't think he needed a Savior.

Then his land deals went south, and his wife left him. He moved, met a girlfriend, and got a job managing a pharmacy. He still didn't need a Savior.

When we met, he'd had a stroke. His money was gone, he had broken up with his girlfriend, and he was estranged from his children. I offered to drive him to church, and he accepted.

One night I brought something to his apartment. He was curled up in bed in a dirty, small apartment, but he said he'd never been happier. Although he didn't have anything, he had Jesus. He needed a Savior.

Do *we* live as though we need a Savior?

We all carry emotional baggage. We may have built up protective walls that isolate us from deep relationships. We may have been hurt or unloved. These experiences affect how we deal with people.

When I'm hurt or put off by someone, the brokenness in our pasts—his and mine—flares between us. God wants us to move past that brokenness and see with compassion.

One Independence Day I was visiting David in a rehab center. They were having a cookout. The outside patio was full of patients. It seemed everyone was either in a cast or a wheelchair. It was very easy to see the physical brokenness in everyone.

It's much more difficult to see interior brokenness.

Do I ignore my own interior brokenness? Do I need a Savior?

*Stuck in a chair,*
*limited mobility,*
*unable to climb.*

*Stuck in addictions,*
*trapped by dependency,*
*unable to break the chains.*

*Stuck in a cell,*
*afraid and scared,*
*unable to break free.*

*Stuck without time,*
*driven by the schedule,*
*unable to hear the silence.*

*Stuck in riches,*
*lavish in our needs,*
*unable to know joy.*

*Stuck in the past,*
*racked with regret,*
*unable to see the vision.*

*Stuck in ourselves,*
*looking for faults,*
*unable to seek goodness.*

*Turn to the light,*
*open your arms,*
*fall with complete trust into freedom.*

# Burden

One day on my morning prayer walk, I realized I was walking fast just to get it over with. I was so consumed with my problems that I was taking this precious time, this gift from God, for granted.

I smiled when I realized God doesn't condemn me for this prideful attitude—he just smiles and waits patiently. When I turn back to him, he wraps his arms around me, his prodigal son.

*When did my walk get so heavy?*
*When did my pace increase?*

*When did I not hear my Lord say,*
*"Can I help you bear the load?"*

*What are these burdens I carry?*
*Am I to proud to let them go?*

*Lord, patiently waiting, offering to help,*
*please show me what I can let go of.*

*Help me give them over.*
*Let me see you gladly accept them out of your love for me.*

*Will I accept that love?*

# Crying for the Connection

On Sundays my mother-in-law and I would bring Communion to David in the nursing home. One day he said a lady named Christine was looking for someone to bring her Communion.

Christine was not in good health. She was very thin and used an oxygen mask. Her only daughter had recently died, and she was emotionally and physically drained. All she wanted was to receive Communion, and her eyes brightened when we brought it to her.

She didn't complain, and she wasn't crying—her faith had taught her that Jesus was all she needed. She had a Savior, and in her hour of deepest need she knew whom to turn to.

*So weak and feeble,*
*she cries out to all who will hear:*
*She craves Communion.*
*Unable to eat or drink,*
*she hungers for her faith*
*and thirsts for the connection*
*in her knowledge of the calling.*

# Consolation

Are you ever exhausted? Have circumstances ever gotten the best of you? Does it look like there is no answer to your struggles?

We have a Savior!

*No longer have I the strength to stand.*
*Beaten down by anxiety, fear, and stress,*
*I fall before you*
*as worries seep from my pores.*
*Rest found in you,*
*the light appears.*
*Your beauty is the focus,*
*consolation is found,*
*lungs filled,*
*legs ready to stand,*
*hands reach skyward,*
*and a heart leaps with joy.*
*Time to pray.*

# Hope

Today, let's allow Jesus to change us.

Isn't hope the root of our desire in the Christian faith? Hope that one day we—our families, friends, everyone—will be in heaven?

How easy it is to lose sight of this hope. If we're not feeling the fruit of the spirit—joy—it's time to refocus that hope.

# Knowledge of the Little

How often we focus on the grand things we hope to accomplish. We admire great works of art, movie stars, politicians, the rich and famous. But do we stop to notice what is in front of us right now?

God designed our world right down to the subatomic particle. Do we appreciate the beauty he gives us each day in the people we encounter, in the sky, the breeze, the sun, the reflections? Do we slow down and enjoy each moment?

My neighbor Rudy, a wonderful man of God, takes close-up pictures of flowers and other elements of nature. He gives each photo a name like Celebration, Humility, or Grace.

Ordinarily I'd pass by these flowers and say they were beautiful, but seeing the magnified, detailed beauty takes my breath away. I can't help but see God's hand in Creation.

Some Sundays after church, I bring Communion to people with Alzheimer's disease. One lady said God had abandoned her. Where was Jesus? Did I really believe in what I was doing?

I said Jesus was with her at that moment. Jesus loves her and will never leave her.

Her eyes lit up as she thanked me with a smile from the depths of her soul. As I started to feel proud of myself for being a great servant of Christ, she said, "Where is Jesus? Why did he leave me?"

Because of her disease, no one would see her profession of faith. Even she may never remember it. But it existed in that moment, and my profession remains with me.

*In the knowledge of the little*
*is found the great pearl.*
*In the wonder of the moment*
*is the fruit of awe.*
*In the seeking of the unnoticed*
*is the enlightened passage.*
*In the glow of his presence,*
*eternal wisdom is claimed.*

# On a Bench of Wood

One early Saturday morning I was attending an event in the city. I walked past a very small park and noticed a clump of blankets on a bench. When it moved, I realized someone had spent the night in the freezing park. I felt sorrow for him, guilt for just passing by, and gratitude for having a safe, warm home. But as I honestly examined my reaction, I realized my initial thoughts had been how dirty and smelly he was.

When another homeless man popped out of a corner and asked me to buy him a cup of coffee, I saw an opportunity to act—to connect and show compassion. I asked him to let me buy him breakfast. When I tried to make conversation, his words didn't make sense. *Should I be afraid? Should I run?*

I hoped that through some connection—a smile or look—he would see that I saw him as a human being and that I did care. And by allowing me to give him a hot meal, he blessed me with a gift in return: The connection of giving and receiving, an eternal connection of love, grace, and humility.

Body in a mound of blankets
stirring on a city bench,
staring me in the face,
filling a glass of pride, disdain, pity, and guilt,
stirring emotions of flight and obligation.
Will I drink this cup?

Wild eyes of unpredictability
dart back and forth,
unable to connect with my world.

A simple offer of the immediate need,
a look into the eyes,
a smile on the lips,
a brief connection of the desire of caring.
This encounter of our souls will be relived.

My brother's situation fulfills a need
in the balance of God's plan.
He makes a sacrifice for me.
Let me not ignore it.
May his dignity touch my soul.

# Let It Go

Think of all the emotions that consume our thoughts: worry, fear, anxiety, anger, pride, and hurt. What good do these bring us? What do we do with them? Do we hold on to them, let them fester? Or do we look at them and ask what is triggering them? *Do I need to let go of that?*

God gave us the precious gift of free will. We have a choice. Will we let our *emotions* consume us, or will we let *God* consume us? Viewing everything through God's perspective is the pathway to holiness.

*O Lord, please help me let go.*

*Let go of bitterness,*
*let in forgiveness.*

*Let go of worry,*
*let in peace.*

*Let go of fear,*
*let in hope.*

*Let go of pride,*
*let in selflessness.*

*Let go of hurt,*
*let in love.*

*Let go of hurriedness,*
*let in this moment.*

*Let go of indifference,*
*let in compassion.*

*Let go of property,*
*let in generosity.*

*Let go of this false self,*
*let in my true self.*

*Let it go,*
*let you grow.*

# Beauty

Nature shows us a power beyond anything humans can do. Its infinite complexity leads us to God.

Whenever I see the Blue Ridge Mountains, I think about how beautiful they are. What is it about mountains that makes us stop and look? Do they make us (and our problems) seem small? Do they make us realize God creates incredible things? Do they make us realize we're part of the plan?

One morning I was unable to go for my morning walk. I told God how much I would miss my time with him that morning. As I walked to my car, I stopped and looked at a beautiful sunrise.

*Moment of beauty,*
*gift of love,*
*shared between a Father and his child.*
*I smile at the beauty of the gift,*
*and the Father smiles back.*
*In that moment we rejoice in*
*his creation, his beauty, his glory, and his love.*
*And it warms my soul.*

# The Beauty of the Forest

I love to sit by a stream or pond and just be with God.
God asks, *What do you see in this moment?*

Possibly it draws me away from thoughts of my
daily duties. Possibly it draws me into this moment
with him. Possibly it shows me what God has created.

Probably it's all of these things and more.

All I know is that God continually surprises me
with his gifts.

*The stream does not worry as it flows down its path.*
*The oak does not waver as it searches for the light.*
*The flower is not proud as it displays its given beauty.*
*The bird is not self-conscious as it sings songs of praise.*
*The forest reflects the beauty designed by your plan.*

# Solemnity of Autumn

As I sat in the woods looking at the remaining autumn leaves, I thought of the blessings I've had. I wondered how I'll feel about my life at the end.

Some elderly people are bitter, focusing only on the times they've been wronged. Some are grateful, focusing on how God brought them through challenges and never deserted them.

We don't suddenly develop these attitudes at the end—we live them every day.

*In the solace of the quiet forest,*
*the season relinquishes its display.*
*Reflection permeates the air.*

*The leaf shines for the last time,*
*its brilliant display turned to rust.*
*The blossom is a fond memory.*

*The knowledge of the seasons has been lived,*
*the good student cherishing the wisdom.*
*The branches smile with understanding.*

*Longing for its home,*
*the grateful soul lets go.*
*In one floating journey, it finds its way back.*

# Soft Breeze

I listened to an audiobook in which the author mentions his love of flowers. Seeing God's beauty in them, he looks for them everywhere. He can be in a meeting, and seeing a picture of a flower on the wall reminds him of God's love.

I have a couple of reminders like that: the sun shining on the water or a soft, gentle breeze. They call me to remember 1 Kings 19:11, about Elijah's encounter with God:

*There was a great wind, so strong that it was splitting mountains and breaking rocks in pieces before the Lord, but the Lord was not in the wind.*

When you encounter these moments, don't ignore them. Stop and give yourself fully to God in that moment.

*Soft breeze, lull me into the silence of knowing. Caress my heart into peaceful submission.*

# Bridge Bench

For years I went to the same park or church for my time alone with God. When I moved, I worried about being away from the places in which I'd encountered God in so many ways.

Then one day I saw a bridge. In the middle of that bridge was a bench, and the sun was shining on it. Taking this as a sign, I took a seat. How many people had traveled this bridge? How many stories and experiences had they lived? God was part of each.

As I travel from one day to the next and from one experience to another, do I reflect on the part God plays in each? Do they lead me toward trusting my future to God? Isn't that the beauty of our lives?

*Smack dab in the middle of an old, rusted bridge— in*
*the middle of the journey from old to new—*
*sits a bench:*
*a place to reflect in the now of God's beauty,*
*a road traveled by all who made this journey,*
*a moment to thank God for the*
*blessings that brought us to this point,*
*a moment of hope in the knowledge of God's fidelity.*

# Closing

Three things I hope you take from this book:

### 1. God Loves You

You can hear the words a thousand times, but until you let God love you by being with him and meditating on him, you will never *know* it. We need to make a practice of contemplating on/in/with him and Scripture. Contemplation isn't reserved for monks.

We must develop an awareness of the love God shares with us in so many beautiful ways each day and cultivate a spirit of gratitude for those gifts.

### 2. Be With Him

Spend time alone with God. Use this little prayer:

> *Beloved, beloved, beloved*
> *Be loved, be loved*
> *Be*

He calls you his beloved. He seeks you, he wants you, he delights in you. Say the word *beloved* until you know this in your soul.

We sometimes focus on our weaknesses—what

we could do better and how we've failed. Well, God doesn't have the same rules we do. Cast those thoughts aside and *be loved*.

After you've felt his calling and known his love, just *be*. You don't have to say or do anything—just sit in his light and love. Carry it with you through your day.

As the father told the older son in the story of the prodigal son, "Son, you are always with me, and all that is mine is yours" (Luke 15:31). God says the same thing to you this day.

*All that is mine is yours.* Think about everything God has. What are those gifts? Peace, joy, compassion, and love.

### 3. *Take Steps of Faith*

All things of spiritual value come from little steps of faith: Hearing a song at church, looking it up online, and listening to it in my car. Hearing a book or quotation that sticks with me and researching it. Passing a church and stopping to pray, even if only for five minutes. Hearing about a need and volunteering. Hearing about a retreat and attending. Questioning an aspect of our faith, researching it, and praying to understand it.

One of the most important aspects of our faith journey is to persevere with patience. We don't have to be perfect. If we know God's love and seek him, he will guide and lead us. He knows what is in our heart. He knows our intent.

God wants to bless us, but do we ask for his blessing each day? The following prayer reminds me to stop, open my heart, ask, and receive God's blessing. It reminds me to eagerly anticipate how his blessings will come to fruition. It reminds me to be grateful for the opportunity to share those blessings.

# Keeper of the Gifts

*Be still and receive my blessing.*
*Open your heart and receive*
*the gift of the unknown,*
*the thought risen,*
*the word spoken,*
*the act of spontaneity—*
*birthed from the spirit of acceptance*
*and housed in the soul.*

I pray this book has been a blessing to you and that it encourages you on your path to holiness.